Introduction

Hi! My name is Kate. I wrote this book when I was eight years old after I went on safari in South Africa. I wrote it with Michelle, my game driver, who taught me so much about animals. In this book you will hear from me and from Michelle. She will teach you all of the things she taught me!

Kate   Michelle

Michelle explained to me that there are many threats to animals, including poaching, and human-wildlife conflict. I didn't know that animals were in danger because of humans.

I came home determined to do something to help the animals of Africa—and guess what— YOU CAN HELP TOO! If we all become animal advocates, we can change the future of these endangered species.

Hop in our truck and come on safari with us!

The authors of *Let's Go On Safari!* are donating 100% of royalties to international organizations who work to protect animals, fight poaching, and promote youth activism.

Let's go on safari!

On the day we left for our safari we got on a really big airplane. After 16 hours, we finally landed in a city called Johannesburg, South Africa.

We met my Godfathers, Bill and Darin, and we all got on a tiny plane that took us to our first lodge. We landed in the middle of the bush!

There wasn't even an airport—just a tiny strip of pavement that a plane could land on!

Guess who greeted us when we got off of the plane?

It was a giraffe family! A mom with her two-week-old baby giraffe stood right at the end of the runway. A truck with no rooftop pulled up and took us to our first lodge.

I was a little nervous, but also excited!

I noticed things were different right away. The roads were all dirt and very bumpy. There were no stop lights, no cars, and no noise — just a single lane road with thick bushes, tall grass, and spiny trees.

We pulled up to our lodge and walked to our tent where we would be sleeping. This was no ordinary tent! It had a wood floor, a porch, and a fancy bathroom with an outdoor shower! On our beds were gifts, including canteens, bug spray, and an animal checklist. That night would be our first game drive.

We unpacked, ate a delicious lunch, and before I knew it, we were officially on safari!

This road is very different from home.

We loved our tent at our first safari camp. Our porch looked right out at the bush.

What do we mean by the "African Bush"?

A *bushveld* is an ecosystem that contains mixed woodland and scrubby grassland. It is an ideal habitat for many different species of plants, animals, and birds.

Many people describe this area as the African bush, and travel on safari to enjoy the beautiful wilderness and to see animals roaming freely.

Kruger National Park, home to some of the most spectacular animals on our planet, is one of the many protected bushveld areas in southern Africa.

The park alone is two million hectares in size. This is equal to the size of New Jersey!

What is a game drive? What items do you find in 4x4 safari trucks?

One of the best ways to enjoy the animals in the bush is to go on a game drive. Game drives take place in 4x4 trucks, and give you the chance to get close to the animals.

You depart in the early mornings or late afternoons to coincide with the cooler times of the day. This is when the animals are most active.

Predators are more active at night, when they move around using darkness as a disguise.

I always bring these items on a game drive:

- Binoculars
- Reference books
- First-aid kit
- Scorpion UV light
- Laser pointer (for looking at stars)
- Camera
- Machete (for cutting back branches)
- Hand sanitizer (to keep clean after touching poop)
- Mosquito repellent
- Sunscreen
- Bush-stop bag (because every tree is a potty!)

5

Exciting things happen at night!

We climbed into our truck and set off down a dirt road. In minutes we saw beautiful birds, a baby rhino with his mom, giraffes, and a herd of elephants! This was my first time to see animals in the wild and not locked up in cages.

Soon we spotted a single female lion on the hunt. Our guide told us this lion had been trying to hunt the same herd of buffalo for over two days. The lion was so skinny from not eating. We watched how focused and determined she was.

We turned off our truck and watched her as she crept closer and closer to the buffaloes. She was only two feet away from us as she stalked the herd so silently. The only sound we could hear was the buffalo munching on the grass in the distance.

All of a sudden, she ran and a cloud of dust filled the air. We heard buffalo hooves running, and we started up our truck to follow the action.

When we came to a clearing we saw the female lion lying on her back, perfectly still …with a baby buffalo in her jaws.

Lions usually live together and hunt in family groups called "prides" but this female was not part of a pride anymore. She had to do all of the work on her own.

She was covering her own scent so she would not get trampled. After about five minutes, the herd left. The lion got up and dragged her kill into the bushes. She knew that hyenas would smell the blood and would come and try to steal it from her.

We pulled our truck next to the bushes she was hiding inside. We watched as she started to eat her dinner. Then, we heard a noise in the distance that sounded like a scream.

We asked our guide what that sound was. It was the hyenas! They could smell the scent of the kill, and they were talking to each other to move in and find the food.

It was almost dark when the hyenas came to where our truck was parked. Two hyenas worked together to try and steal the buffalo away from the lion.

Wow, did she put up a fight! I have never heard such growling and screaming coming from animals. We saw the lion swipe and scratch the nose of a hyena, but another

hyena got part of the buffalo. Then the hyenas started fighting each other for the belly of the dead buffalo! Finally, one of them ran away with it.

In the end, the single female lion did get most of her meal. I was happy for her, because she had spent such a long time hunting without any help from a pride. When we got back to our tent that night, we could hear hyenas calling in the distance.

I knew that meant that some wild animal was getting to eat, that some animal had been killed, and that the hyenas were on their way to get any scraps. I could not wait until morning to see more!

Why are some lions part of a pride — and some not?

Lions are social animals and are usually found in a pride. However, there can be a number of reasons that a lioness is on her own. She may have lost all the members in her pride or somehow become detached.

Perhaps she separated herself because she had cubs. Or, she was too old or sick to keep up with the pride and is now alone. Lionesses in a pride will hunt strategically together, but a lone lioness is still capable of being a successful hunter.

How do lions and hyenas interact?

Hyenas and lions are eternal enemies and will fight bitterly over a carcass. One of the biggest drawbacks a lone lioness will face in the wild is not having the safety in numbers that a pride would provide, thus reducing her ability to protect herself and her kills. One-on-one, a lioness will likely win the battle. Against a clan of hyenas, her chances are slim.

Hyenas are animals with amazing senses of hearing, sight, and smell—they can smell a carcass from miles away! Hyenas often patrol their territories alone, listening for the distress calls of animals or the sounds of predators feeding on a carcass.

Hyenas are quick to call for backup if they need it, using one of 14 different contact calls. A whoop, squeal, growl, or giggle each communicates different information to the rest of the clan.

Hyenas have their cubs in an underground den. They are black when they are born and only emerge from the den at four weeks of age. They start to develop spots when they are three months old.

Learning about footprints.

Our phone rang at 5 a.m. for our morning game drive. Michelle met us at our tent with coffee, hot chocolate, and cookies to help wake us up. She asked, "How do you think you find the animals out in the bush?" I answered, "You hear them, and then you follow them!"

True, sometimes you hear animals—but most of the time you look down on the ground to find your way. We spent time staring at the dirt road. I was surprised to find so many clues on the ground.

When a footprint is shiny, that means the track is new and the animal is not far away. If the track is covered in dust and not shiny, that means the animal was there a long time ago and has moved on.

We learned to look at the ground closely. By the end of the day, we could tell if a print was from a hyena or a lion. We learned the difference between an elephant and rhino print!

We put our tracking knowledge to the test. We saw a shiny set of prints from a leopard family. We looked at the ways the branches were bending, and we drove into the bush. We had to duck so that trees would not hit us in the face. Finally, we found a den where the momma leopard lived with her two cubs.

We sat and watched them play, and I was super proud of my animal tracking skills.

What can you learn from animal tracks?

There are times on game drives when you drive for hours and don't see any animals, making you wonder if they even exist! The problem is, if you don't know what to look for you will never find them. This is where tracks and signs come in.

The bush is full of information and messages — you just need to know how to read the language!

Tracks on the ground, broken branches, mud on leaves — even poop can tell you a story! From a single footprint you can tell who was there, the species of animal, its gender and age, the direction of movement, what it was doing, how long ago it walked there, and sometimes even their mood! Porcupines, for example, drag their quills on the ground when they are relaxed. When they are stressed, their quills point up and you don't see any trace of them.

Did you know that poop can tell a story?

Once I was walking in the bush following elephant tracks when I came across fresh elephant poop. The dung looked more like a pile of leaves than poop! Elephants are known to have very poor digestive systems—they process only about 40% of their food. But the amount of intact vegetation in this pile of poop was unusual.

After some thought, a clue about this elephant became clear. In old age, elephant teeth become ground down and some end up with no teeth at all. This makes chewing food extremely difficult and leads to malnutrition. In this case, the dung alerted us to the fact that this elephant we were following was very old!

How can you get so close to wild animals?

One question that everyone asks me is, "How can you get so close to a lion, an elephant, or a rhino and they don't jump right into your truck?" The truth is I have no idea why we are safe in the truck, but for some reason, these animals respect the vehicle and do not see it as a threat.

Our guide told us if we stuck our hands out of the doors or if we stood up, the animals would notice something different and might change their behavior. It is hard to believe that when we drive up to an animal, the noise of the truck does not scare them. In fact, if an animal is sleeping and we drive up next to them, sometimes they don't even wake up!

If we got out of our truck, and just our tiny pinky toe touched the ground, an animal could sense the vibrations — and might either run away or attack!

Our noisy truck did not disturb this cat . . . taking a nap!

What do we mean by "animal habituation"?

"Habituating" animals to vehicles and to people allows them to become familiar with different sounds and smells. Eventually, animals no longer fear trucks on safari. This requires careful and respectful interaction.

As guides, we watch the behavior of animals very carefully. The most important thing to remember is that animals are unpredictable and may be happy and relaxed one moment, and upset in another. As a guide, it is our job to read their body language.

Sometimes animals are happy for you to sit and watch them. Other times they are not. When an animal is agitated, the ethical thing to do is leave them alone.

Animals have comfort zones. One is the *alert zone,* where they are aware of your presence but do not feel threatened and continue with their natural activities.

The *warning zone* comes next, when the animal feels that you are too close and will warn you by growling, shaking their head, or swishing their tail aggressively.

The final zone is the *critical zone.* If you don't respect the animals' communication and continue to get closer, one of two things will happen — they will either run away or they will fight to protect themselves because you have scared them.

Can you tell what comfort zone these animals are in?

Hip, Hip, Hooray!

We packed up our things and moved around to different lodges. One lodge was on a lake with hippos right outside of our bathroom window! I've never seen so many hippos snorting and splashing—they make the funniest sounds! There was a baby hippo—I named him Hippy.

I don't see how hippos get so big, because they only eat grass. When it is hot during the day, hippos will stay in the water because they have very sensitive skin. Hippos can even get sunburned!

Did you know that hippos can smell under water?

Hippos have an organ in the roof of their mouth called the Jacobson's Organ which detects pheromones (chemical messages) through a combination of smell and taste. Hippos use this information to learn about other hippos around them, like their moods and behaviors. Most mammals have a Jacobson's organ, but hippos are the only ones who can use it under water!

What is "poaching"?

On safari, I learned that the animals we spent time watching were in danger of someone trying to kill them for their body parts.

This is called *poaching,* and it makes me sad to think about certain species being extinct forever. How could anybody kill an elephant or a rhino and leave a baby without its mom? Poaching is cruel and must be stopped.

This young lion and baby elephant were both caught in snares. Look how swollen the elephant's leg is. Without treatment, both animals would die from infection. Both of these animals were found, treated by vets, and survived thanks to the Bumi Hills Foundation.

What is a "snare"?

A *snare* is a thin wire tied to trees or bushes that catch and kill animals indiscriminately as they walk by. Even if an animal escapes the trap, they are often left still tangled in the wire. This causes life-threatening wounds and infection.

Look at the terrible damage that a snare can cause!

These snares were found and removed before an animal could get hurt.

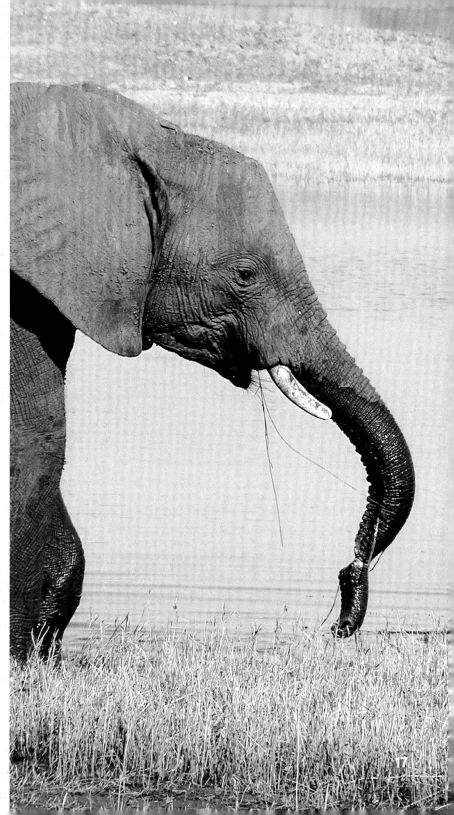

What animals are most in danger of being killed by poachers?

Rhinoceros

A rhino's horn is made of keratin — the same thing that your fingernails are made of! Rhinos are in terrible danger of becoming extinct, as people kill them for this horn. In some places, people think the horn can be used as medicine and for some it is seen as a sign of wealth and success.

Pangolins

Pangolins are shy, harmless animals that are covered in scales and have a long, sticky tongue to slurp up ants and termites. The Pangolin is the world's most trafficked mammal because of myths about their scales' ability to cure rare illnesses. It is estimated that up to 2.7 million pangolins are removed from the wild EVERY year.

Hippopotamus

Recently, poachers have turned their attention to hunting hippos for the ivory in their teeth. Now hippos are at great risk.

Elephants

Records show that about 55 elephants die EACH DAY from poaching. People hunt elephants for their large tusks which are made of ivory. Ivory can be worth over $1,000 per pound in certain parts of the world.

Leopards

Leopards have disappeared from 40% of their territories in Africa, placing this elusive cat on the nearly threatened list. Poachers kill leopards for their beautiful furs, which are often used to make coats and ceremonial robes.

Lions

In the last two decades, lion populations have plummeted 42% throughout Africa. The 20,000 or fewer lions that remain now face ever-increasing pressures from poaching, habitat loss, and conflict with humans. Illegal trade in lion bones and body parts such as whiskers and tails for use in traditional medicines are also a major threat to the species survival.

What is human-wildlife conflict?

A serious problem in Africa is *human-wildlife conflict*. As local populations and communities grow and expand, natural wild spaces are reduced, leaving people and wildlife competing for space, food, and water.

As shared resources grow scarcer, the conflict between humans and animals increases! Wild animals might attack livestock or raid crops for food, and humans might attack the wildlife in retaliation. This can have deadly results on both sides.

Bee-lieve it or not:
A tiny bee can save an elephant!

Farmers and villagers in Africa plant crops to feed their families—just like the gardens we plant at our homes. Imagine if a giant elephant came along and started munching on your garden! This is what happens in Africa. When a farmer or villager depends on this crop to feed their family, this becomes a problem. Sometimes a farmer will try and kill the elephant with a spear in order to save his crops.

Animal experts discovered that elephants are TERRIFIED of bees! Organizations started building bee boxes along fences to keep elephants from coming too close to crops. As the elephants get close, they knock the fence causing the bee hives to shake and swing. This makes the bees inside get mad and swarm! The elephants hear the bees buzzing and turn to run away before they get stung. It is hard to believe that a tiny insect can save a giant elephant!

21

There are many people working to save animals. They need your support!

Rangers of the Bumi Hills Foundation look for snares and signs of poachers as they patrol the Lake Kariba region of Zimbabwe. You can adopt a ranger and be a part of the team that saves wildlife! Visit **www.bumihillsfoundation.org** to learn more.

Global Wildlife Conservation
Austin, Texas USA

Kate is proud that Global Wildlife Conservation (GWC) is headquartered in her hometown of Austin, Texas! If you love science, this an organization you will want to learn more about. GWC boasts top scientists who are saving species and habitats in every corner of the globe.

Did you know that there is a species of rhino called the Javan Rhino? Today, there are only 68 Javan Rhinos left in the world. The animals are found only in Ujung Kulon National Park in Java, Indonesia. This rhino is so rare, very few photos have ever been taken of them!

GWC is working with local and international partners to save the Javan Rhino by protecting their home, promoting mating, and reducing disease. To learn more about the Javan Rhino, and to learn fascinating facts about turtles, tapirs, monkeys, frogs, and even a mysterious Asian Unicorn, visit GWC's website: www.globalwildlife.org.

Once ranging from the foothills of the Himalayas to the islands of Indonesia, now there are only 68 Javan Rhinos left in the world. This is a rare picture of this endangered animal.

Photo: Robin Moore/GWC

The David Sheldrick Wildlife Trust

Kenya, East Africa

There is a special place in Kenya that gives orphaned baby elephants—ones that have lost their families— a chance to recover and grow up to become wild elephants. This place is called The David Sheldrick Wildlife Trust (DSWT). Every day of the year The DSWT is on call, traveling on land and in airplanes, rescuing orphaned elephants and other wildlife that are alone with no hope of survival. The DSWT has successfully raised over 230 orphans (150 of these are now living in the wild), and some of these elephants have gone on to have babies of their own!

When a baby elephant arrives at The DSWT, he or she receives around-the-clock care from a Keeper. The Keepers provide constant love and support to the baby. The Keepers even sleep with the baby elephants in their stalls! Baby elephants stay in the nursery from one to three years and then they graduate to another part of Kenya to continue their journey to the wild.

Did you know infant elephants are milk dependent for at least THREE years?

The DSWT created a special milk formula to help them survive. The formula has to be mixed in just the right way to give the elephants all of the nutrients they need to grow big and strong.

The DSWT believes that kids can help to be a part of the solution to save elephants from extinction. Here are ways that you, your family, and your friends can help:

Foster an Elephant from The DSWT.

For $50 a year you can foster an orphaned elephant of your choice and watch them grow and eventually return to the wild! Be creative—you can raise $50 really fast! When you foster you get monthly updates on your elephant, including access to diary entries from their Keeper, photos, videos, and a monthly watercolor painting from CEO Angela Sheldrick. You can watch your baby elephant grow up and feel like you are in Africa!

Say "No" to buying anything with ivory, and tell everyone you know to do the same.

We highly recommend that your family follow The DSWT on Instagram. The daily photos and videos of the baby elephants racing to their milk bottles and splashing in their mud baths will make your day! You can find The DSWT on Instagram @DSWT.

To learn more about The DSWT and to foster your baby elephant, go to www.sheldrickwildlifetrust.org.

The Jane Goodall Institute

Vienna, Virginia USA

The Jane Goodall Institute (JGI) is a global community conservation organization that advances the vision and work of Dr. Jane Goodall. By protecting chimpanzees and other great apes, while inspiring people to conserve the natural world we all share, JGI improves the lives of people, other animals, and the environment. You can find out more about JGI and support their work by visiting janegoodall.org.

JGI also has a youth service program called Roots & Shoots! Created in 1991 by Dr. Jane Goodall, JGI's Roots & Shoots program is for young people of all ages—from kindergarten through college! The mission is to foster respect and compassion for all living things, to promote understanding of all cultures and beliefs, and to inspire every individual to take action to make the world a better place for people, other animals, and the environment.

Roots & Shoots empowers young people (like YOU) to become the type of compassionate citizens who will make choices that build a better world. Through the program, youth lead local change through service learning projects while developing skills and traits of compassionate leaders. Hundreds of thousands of Roots & Shoots members all over the world are working to improve their communities and be the kinds of compassionate citizens our world needs. Together, the actions taken by each individual weave together to create a tapestry of hope.

Join JGI's Roots & Shoots today!
Here's what to do:

1. With permission from a parent or caregiver, join Roots & Shoots by signing up at rootsandshoots.org.

2. Start making a difference right away. Get in on a one-click campaign that excites you and creates a positive impact by visiting www.rootsandshoots.org/campaigns. You can also get inspired and join the Roots & Shoots community by following @rootsandshoots on Facebook, Instagram and Twitter.

3. Find out how Roots & Shoots youth are changing the world. You can learn all about the projects that are shaping our world for the better by visiting JGI's Good For All News blog! Check them out and get project ideas at news.janegoodall.org/category/youth-power.

4. Find a group or form your own Roots & Shoots team. Once you have your group, or are working solo, design your own service campaign to address the issues that YOU care most about. Follow the four-step formula for identifying a Roots & Shoots campaign that speaks to YOU. The step-by-step instructions are easy to follow at www.rootsandshoots.org/formula.

(Clockwise from top left)

Jane Goodall watches orphan chimpanzee Wounda after her release on Tchindzoulou Island.
Photo Credit: the Jane Goodall Institute

Dr. Jane Goodall with a group of Roots & Shoots members in Salzburg, Austria.
Photo Credit: Robert Ratzer

In the early days of her chimpanzee studies, Jane Goodall lived in a tent and typed up her field notes each night by the light of a lantern.
Photo Credit: the Jane Goodall Institute

Kids Can Help Save Animals!
Here are some stories to inspire you.

Kate (the co-author of *Let's Go on Safari!*) sells smoothies and lemonade on weekends and donates the money to charities that help save animals from extinction.

10-year-old gorilla advocate, Addy from Maryland, has raised thousands of dollars for the Dian Fossey Gorilla Fund. Here, Addy is hosting a Gorilla Gala!

Student members of Malihai Clubs (youth conservation clubs) in Tanzania show off artwork, highlighting human-wildlife conflict, and help educate others in their schools about wildlife protection efforts. This project was supported by the Singita Grumeti Fund.

You can make a difference! Every kid can do something to help!

Advocate: A person who publicly supports a particular cause.

An advocate works to influence others about something they care about. Kate has decided to focus on animals. You can pick from a variety of topics, including: recycling, helping the homeless, or preserving the oceans.

You can make a difference if you lead by example.

Take action. Show the world—starting with your friends, family, and neighbors—that you care.

Here are a few ideas to help you get started:

1. Design a poster to teach others about your cause. Ask your teacher if you can present it to your class at school.

2. Create a service learning project that helps people, other animals, and the environment by joining the Jane Goodall Institute's Roots & Shoots program.

3. Foster a baby elephant from The DSWT with your family.

4. Pick a wildlife organization that you discovered in this book, such as Global Wildlife Conservation, and think how you can make an impact and support it.

Kids can make a difference! We hope this book inspires you and gives you good ideas of things to do.

Making a new friend in Africa.

I have many special memories about Africa, but the best part was meeting Michelle.

Michelle always let me do extra special things. On one game drive, she let me sit in the front with her! We spotted a bull elephant, and Michelle asked if I wanted to use the radio to call in our sighting. I picked up the radio, pushed the button and said, "There is a bull elephant north of the airstrip." I felt like a real guide!

Michelle explained to me that it was her job to call in all animal sightings to track their movements and monitor their behavior. I will never forget when Michelle turned to me and said, "Kate, I have a surprise for you." We drove for 20 minutes and then stopped. She said, "Kate, look over there."

And that's when I saw it—my first ever cheetah! He was standing on a tree that had fallen, and he was *chirping!* Yes, cheetahs chirp like a bird! Michelle said he was probably calling out to his mate. We sat and watched the cheetah while Michelle explained that there are fewer than 7,000 cheetah left in the wild.

Thank You

Kate would like to thank the following people for helping her with this book:

Michelle — Thank you for teaching me so many things about the animals of Africa. Thank you for working to help keep these animals safe. Thank you for writing this book with me!

Bill and Darin — Thank you for traveling to Africa with me and making this safari so fun. Thank you for sharing your amazing photos in my book.

Trinity Episcopal School — Thank you for your support with my book project. Thank you for organizing and hosting the "Trinity Kids Editing Panel."

Members of the Trinity Kids Editing Panel include: Caroline H., Hudson L., Tej D., Emme K., Harrison H., Elise B., Will G., and Hampton C.

Friends — Thank you for sharing your ideas and thoughtful edits on my book. These friends include: Spencer H., Kate S., Sierra S., Greer M., Sophia H., Emme L., Jennifer L., Julie G., Avery B., and Victoria R.

Meg Renwick — Thank you to my favorite art teacher for creating the incredible bee and elephant drawings in my book.

Animal advocates — Thank you for caring for animals and doing everything you can to save them. I hope you will adopt an elephant from The DSWT and I hope you will join Roots & Shoots! Don't let anybody tell you that you are too young to make a difference. Advocacy knows no age limit!

Meet safari guide Michelle Campbell.

Hello! Welcome to my wild and wonderful world! I was born in South Africa and lived in five different countries growing up. I fell in love with the bush at age seven when my family took me on safari. I never forgot that experience and years later, whilst working as an economist, I decided to follow my dream to become a safari guide.

My favourite thing about guiding is being in the bush and learning new things about wildlife, and sharing that with families! The more you know about animals, the more fascinating they are! Hearing the whoop of a hyena, roar of a lion, or that deep rumble from an elephant excites me every time!

I left my job as a guide and moved into my Land Rover. That's right—I lived out of a truck! For 393 days, I travelled the continent of Africa volunteering for wildlife projects, from anti-poaching, conservation education, to wildlife rehabilitation. I wanted to learn as much as possible about what different people were doing to help save animals and most importantly, how I could make an impact.

I learned a lot on my 393 day expedition. Today, I work with families all around the world, connecting them with hands-on conservation experiences in Africa. Together, you and I can go on an exciting adventure, just like I did with Kate. Let's roll up our sleeves and help save animals! From collaring an elephant for research to bottle feeding baby rhinos—our advocacy has no limit!

It's my life mission to make a meaningful contribution to conservation. Would you and your family like to join me? Let's go on safari together and do what we can to help save animals from extinction!

Crickhollow Books is an imprint of Great Lakes Literary, based in Milwaukee, Wisconsin, an independent press publishing quality fiction and nonfiction.

www.KidsCanSaveAnimals.com

Let's Go On Safari!
© 2019, Kate Gilman Williams and Michelle Campbell

ISBN: 978-1-933987-27-9

Summary: What happens when Kate, an 8-year-old girl, meets Michelle, a professional wildlife guide, while on safari in South Africa? The girls turn their adventures into a book encouraging a young generation to advocate for animals! *Let's Go On Safari!* invites children and families to hop in a truck, experience the thrill of a safari, and discover how they can save endangered animals along the way. Kate Gilman Williams and Michelle Campbell are donating all royalties to three leading international organizations who work to protect animals, fight poaching, and promote youth activism. Royalties will be donated to The David Sheldrick Wildlife Trust (33%), the Jane Goodall Institute (33%), and Global Wildlife Conservation (33%). Kate and Michelle prove that advocacy has no age limit and that kids can help save animals on the brink of extinction.

BISAC Codes

JNF003270   JUVENILE NONFICTION / Animals / Endangered
JNF038010   JUVENILE NONFICTION / People & Places / Africa
JNF037020   JUVENILE NONFICTION / Science & Nature / Environmental Conservation & Protection

First Crickhollow Books Edition
Printed in the USA

Photo Credits

Cover photo (cheetah) by Wild Wonderful World.

Inside front cover (adult and baby rhino) by Wild Wonderful World.

Photo p.7 (hyena silhouette) by Wild Wonderful World, additional photos p.7 (lion and hyenas) by Mike Williams.

Photos pp. 8 – 12 by Wild Wonderful World.

Photos p.16 (injured lion and elephant) courtesy Bumi Hills Foundation, used by permission.

Photo p.18 (pangolin) courtesy DepositPhotos.

Graphic illustrations p.20 and 21 (elephant and bee, and diagrams of bee boxes) by Meg Renwick, used by permission.

Photo p.22 (rangers on patrol) by Bumi Hills Foundation, used by permission.

Photo p.23 (Javan Rhino) by Robin Moore of Global Wildlife Conservation, used by permission.

Photo p.24 (man feeding baby DSWT elephant) by Kate Gilman Williams.

Photos p.27 courtesy the Jane Goodall Institute, used by permission.

Photo p.28 (students of Malihai Clubs) by Wild Wonderful World.

Photos p.29 (baby cheetahs at play), courtesy DepositPhotos.

Inside back cover (muddy rhino) by Wild Wonderful World.

Back cover photo (Kate and Michelle in vehicle) by Darin Severns.

Additional wildlife and landscape photography by Bill Huffaker, Darin Severns and Wild Wonderful World.

This book is dedicated to Philip Martin, for being the kind of person who first gave a voice to a little girl with big dreams.